# Arachnids

LEVEL 10

# Teaching Tips

## White Level 10

This book focuses on developing reading independence, fluency, and comprehension.

## Before Reading

- Ask readers what they think the book will be about based on the title. Have them support their answer.

## Read the Book

- Encourage readers to read silently on their own.
- As readers encounter unfamiliar words, ask them to look for context clues to see if they can figure out what the words mean. Encourage them to locate boldfaced words in the glossary and ask questions to clarify the meaning of new vocabulary.
- Allow readers time to absorb the text and think about each chapter.
- Ask readers to write down any questions they have about the book's content.

## After Reading

- Ask readers to summarize the book.
- Encourage them to point out anything they did not understand and ask questions.
- Ask readers to review the questions on page 23. Have them go back through the book to find answers. Have them write their answers on a separate sheet of paper.

© 2024 Booklife Publishing
This edition is published by arrangement with Booklife Publishing.

North American adaptations © 2024 Jump!
5357 Penn Avenue South
Minneapolis, MN 55419
www.jumplibrary.com

Decodables by Jump! are published by Jump! Library.
All rights reserved. No part of this book may be reproduced in any form without written permission from the publisher.

Library of Congress Cataloging-in-Publication Data
is available at www.loc.gov or upon request from
the publisher.

ISBN: 979-8-88524-802-0 (hardcover)
ISBN: 979-8-88524-803-7 (paperback)
ISBN: 979-8-88524-804-4 (ebook)

## Photo Credits

Images are courtesy of Shutterstock.com. With thanks to Getty Images, Thinkstock Photo and iStockphoto. Cover – Eric Isselee. p4–5 –Alex Stemmer, Yuvan aves. p6–7 -Audrey Snider-Bell, torook. p8–9 – Kurt Hohenbichler, Paul Looyen. p10–11 – Art Wittingen, Kopiyka. p12–13 – LorraineHudgins, Tom Wurl. p14–15 –Henrik Larsson, Ian Scammell. p16–17 - Gabi Wolf, Henrik Larsson. p18–19 - Joy Ondreicka, guentermanaus. p20–21 - Lamyai, Alex Stemmer, stevenku.

# Table of Contents

Page 4     Arachnids

Page 6     Body Parts

Page 10    Getting Around

Page 12    Predators and Prey

Page 14    Adaptation

Page 16    Life Cycles

Page 18    Extreme Arachnids

Page 22    Index

Page 23    Questions

Page 24    Glossary

# Arachnids

Arachnids have been around for 400 million years and inhabit every continent on Earth except Antarctica. It is estimated that there are 90,000 **species** of arachnids, including spiders, crabs, and scorpions. Arachnids live in all kinds of habitats, including forests, deserts, rain forests, swamps, and mountains.

Unlike insects, which have six legs and three segments to their bodies, arachnids have eight legs and two segments: a head and an abdomen. Most arachnids lay eggs, but scorpions give birth to live young.

ARACHNID CHECKLIST
- No backbone
- Cold-blooded
- Most lay eggs
- Two body segments
- Eight legs
- Exoskeleton (skeleton outside the body)

# Body Parts

## Exoskeleton

Arachnids have a hard outer layer called an exoskeleton, which supports and protects them from the outside. An exoskeleton cannot get bigger, so as an arachnid grows, it grows a new, larger exoskeleton and **molts** out of the old one.

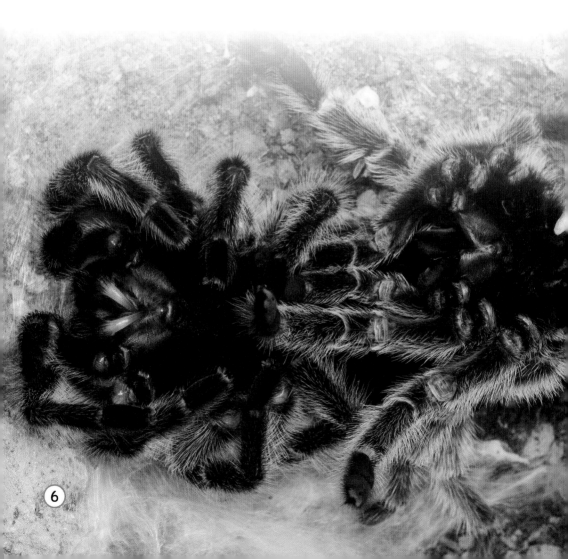

## Legs

Arachnids have jointed legs. The exoskeleton is stiff and cannot bend, so jointed legs help an arachnid move quickly and skillfully. Arachnids have 48 knees—six on each of their eight legs! If a leg is broken, a new one grows between molts.

Tarantula

## Spinnerets

Spiders have organs called spinnerets on the undersides of their abdomens. They use spinnerets to spin silk. The silk is squeezed out through tiny holes in the spinnerets. In the air, the silk becomes sticky and is used to make webs and cocoons for eggs.

Wasp spider's spinneret weaving a web

## The Front Segment

The front segment of an arachnid's body contains its eyes, stomach, brain, mouth, fangs, and **venom** glands. All eight legs are attached to the front segment.

Spiders usually have eight eyes, but most have very poor eyesight.

# Getting Around

Arachnids move by walking, running, jumping, and even swimming. Spiders move using hydraulics. This means that they use liquid under pressure to create power where it is needed. While two pairs of legs are in the air, the other two pairs are on the ground for support.

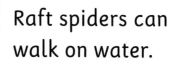

Raft spiders can walk on water.

Spiders can run up walls and across ceilings thanks to over 500,000 tiny hairs called setules found on the ends of their legs.

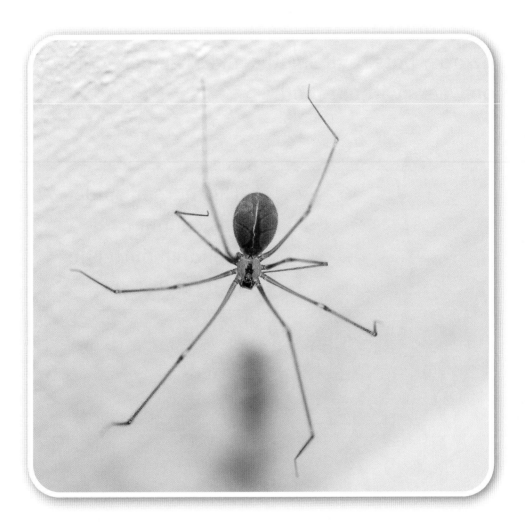

Some spiders travel by ballooning. This is when a spider climbs very high and then releases lots of silk into the wind, which carries the spider.

# Predators and Prey

Most arachnids eat other animals. Spiders eat a variety of insects, while tarantulas eat frogs, mice, and birds. Larger tarantulas also eat lizards, bats, and small snakes. Spiders can go weeks without food.

This garden spider has caught a monarch butterfly in its web.

Animals that hunt spiders include monkeys, birds, and centipedes. The tarantula hawk, which is actually a wasp, is a predator that hunts tarantulas in their **burrows**. It paralyzes the tarantula with a sting, then drags it to its own burrow to feed its young.

A tarantula hawk with its paralyzed **prey**

# Adaptation

Arachnids have adapted to their environments in many amazing ways. Adaptation helps a species survive by enabling animals to cope with extreme conditions and ward off **predators**. Crab spiders can **camouflage** themselves by changing color to match their environment.

This goldenrod crab spider is perfectly camouflaged on a dandelion.

Most scorpions live in hot, dry deserts. Scorpions have adapted to live in this environment. Food is hard to come by in the desert, so scorpions have adapted to be able to go without food for up to a year!

This emperor scorpion is eating its prey.

# Life Cycles

Before **mating**, male arachnids do special things. For example, this might involve special movements, such as rocking their bodies back and forth. A male spider pulls on the female's web in a particular way so that she knows he is a mate rather than her dinner!

Female spiders are much bigger than male spiders and often eat the male after mating.

Almost all female spiders spin an egg sac out of silk to protect their eggs. Some hide the egg sac under a rock or attach it to a plant. Some species carry the egg sac on their bodies. These **spiderlings** then ride on their mother's back until they are ready to leave her.

Spiderling

# Extreme Arachnids

## Black Widow Spider

Black widow spiders are some of the most venomous spiders in the world. The females have red or orange hourglass shapes on their abdomens, while males have red or pink spots. Their bite is thought to be 15 times more venomous than a rattlesnake's.

## Goliath Birdeater

The Goliath birdeater is the largest spider in the world by weight. It can defend itself by rubbing the hairs on its body together to make a hissing sound. It can also send out a shower of spiked hairs from its abdomen that ward off predators.

Female Goliath birdeaters can live for up to 20 years.

## Emperor Scorpion

The emperor scorpion has hairs on its pincers and tail. These hairs pick up vibrations in the air and on the ground, helping the scorpion discover prey. Scorpions glow a blueish green under UV light. Scientists think this glow may ward off predators but also attract insects as prey.

## Dust Mites

Although we cannot see them, dust mites share our homes with us. Every 24 hours, the average human loses 1 million dead skin cells. These cells provide food for dust mites. Dust mites suck water out of the air, so humid places make ideal habitats.

Dust mite

# Index

eyes 9
heads 5
legs 5, 7, 9–11
mites 21
scorpions 4–5, 15, 20

spiders 4, 8–14, 16–19
spinnerets 8
webs 8, 12, 16

## How to Use an Index

An index helps us find information in a book. Each word has a set of page numbers. These page numbers are where you can find information about that word.

Page numbers

Example: balloons 5, 8–10, 19

Important word

This means page 8, page 10, and all the pages in between.
Here, it means pages 8, 9, and 10.

# Questions

1. How many legs do arachnids have?

2. What is the largest spider in the world by weight?

3. What are baby spiders called?

4. Can you use the Table of Contents to find information about how arachnids get around?

5. Can you use the Index to find dust mites in the book?

6. Using the Glossary, can you define what molting is?

# Glossary

**burrows:**
Tunnels or holes in the ground made or used as homes.

**camouflage:**
To disguise something so that it blends in with its surroundings.

**mating:**
Joining together to produce babies.

**molts:**
Loses an old exoskeleton so that a new one can grow.

**predators:**
Animals that hunt other animals for food.

**prey:**
An animal that is hunted by another animal for food.

**species:**
One of the groups into which similar animals and plants are divided.

**spiderlings:**
Young spiders.

**venom:**
Poison produced by some snakes and spiders.